MW01167292

SOCIAL SUICIDE

Copyright ©2018
Angela Crandall

All rights reserved. This book contains material protected under International and Federal Copyright Laws and Treaties. Any unauthorized reprint or use of this material is prohibited. No part of this book may be reproduced or transmitted in any form or by any means, electronic or mechanical, including photocopying, recording, or by any information storage and retrieval system without express written permission from the author / publisher

Paperback Edition
* Published as Poetic Puzzle Pieces (Social Suicide) e-book. This edition contains bonus material.

Angelada books

ISBN-13:978-0692130933

ISBN-10:0692130934

Kindle Edition

ASIN- BOOKGR2SG6

First Edition

Cover design by Toni Kerr/Angela K. Crandall

There are those who will make you question what is real.
Time and again, forcing you to second guess yourself.
Then one or two who will bring the glorious light out
from within you.
Teaching you how to define your power.

This poetry book is dedicated to the Misunderstood, the Punk Rocker, the Emo, the kid who sits alone at lunch. All those who feel others have placed them in isolation just remember, keep hope in your heart, destiny in hand, and keep on dreaming. Hold fast to the loyalty you have unto you, and stay true to yourself. It is a world of illusions, and beauty before you. One filled with hope, but also darkness don't let them steal your smile, bright star, or the child within you. Instead, use your happiness, find your balance, and be one with what, or who makes you-YOU.

Introduction

Writing has always been as important to me as the music I listen to, the stories I read, and information I receive on television, News, Radio, and basic media. I use to keep a journal on my life, daily goals, issues, concerns, but I have found poetry to be more pleasant. I can discuss things without giving away a lot of information that may be unnecessary, and or views veiled. People like me; we hide behind our words at times afraid. I don't find myself to always fear analysis of others depending on whose presence I am in. There are times I let all my defenses fall. I'd find warmth if I could let everyone inside.
The problem is, a long time ago I shared a secret with friends Something I used as a survival skill to keep from plummeting into depression.
This is what caught my sleeve
A rip, a tare, a cutout from within
Bringing me down from the comfort it brought me
Took me to realize I should have kept it
Not given it away so easily
Why I even wanted to share in what it was, now astonishes me, but I thought it would be OK.
It wasn't
I've always liked words, they don't bite back if they are your own.
Granted, they won't hug you, or hold you.
Thoughts, expressions they make you smirk,
Invoke silhouettes of comfort, or seem real even when they are not.
I wonder what those girls think of me now, with the knowledge of my secret
Burning on their tongues
Who'd they wag it to?
Groups and clusters would gather as I sat alone in those days

Until I proved that I shun what once was part of me
Admitting the fault it had, dropped out, non-truth
Creation
What are we if not what we have created; brought forth, made
real what was once factitious.

Part One:

Fallen

Isolation

Claim acceptance, but then turn a blind eye to circumstance. Words, spoken are different from actions seen. I sit in a chair with my head on my desk; breathing in the wood, cool on my face closing my eyes, darkness lived each day. Proven facts, - Hold- Realism lets one down as fantasy creates a safe haven Shunned. Safe arms surround me not afraid to pull me close. I have heard people say freedom lies within our mind, the place we can travel, people we can visit, worlds created in an unacceptable manner. A form of solitude found yet not enough. You hurt even more knowing the impossibility of it all. I saw sadness in your eyes when you could not make it all better. When a wand simply would not swish it away. Peace found only within one's self not others for they cannot make peace with who I am, or how I see.

Looking up I stare at a face. One who showed me truth, without physical existence beyond an image seen reflecting me. I don't need to shake her hand, although it would be monumental. I only need to know she is still here. I pick my head up from the wooden table slowly standing up as not to fall from my place steadying myself to lean against the wall behind me glaring at the poster with a tear streaked face. No one wants to see your sadness, fears, and depleting sense of hope melting from your eyes dear. I need to lie down. I go over to my bed, grabbing the teddy bear sitting beside an overstuffed chair. It's time to dream, to sit cross legged, to define myself without their definition of sanity. I lay down on my bed, wrap my arms around my bear, to go to a place they wish me to deceive, but which they feel deceives me, into a place I will never be rejected. You speak, open wide, and with pleasure, they say "NOTHING HAS CHANGED." Then you see it in how they hold you away from them while you hug, pat you on the back due to fear, thoughts that just might be going through your head. The only comfort to

you is the Queen herself, or a beautiful person who only exists in the land of another realm. Once I'm lucid hoping for dreams that will lather me in serene still like waters not many places can this be achieved waiting for the day, when no longer will you question my motives, able to see behind the mask you wear, letting it cover your eyes, wishing you could look through mine to see you have nothing to fear.
I am sleeping.

Life Cycle

As time passes, I pass too
Like dust in the wind,
A grain of sand on a shore.
My hopes all about the Earth.
The kindness I wish to scatter,
Amongst all
Will be what I leave behind
When I fall
From my sense of self
There will be none.

Stolen

Be careful what you say,
Someone might be listening
Watching, hoping you'll screw
Up to fit in that box,
The one you were assumed to be
Opinions, accusations, judgments of your
Character on acts of anger.
The many different you's
Including ones that just stumble onto the
Pavement,
The character you never knew stood right beside
Inside you
Laying down the dark path
Littered with trees, falling asleep in silence
Beneath the stars
Surviving, smiling, losing control of
All of who I am just to be,
Still it is there an accident waiting
To happen.

Attempt

Walking along the shore
Emptiness, grows inside
Waves lap rigged stones
My pride rises, and falls
The ground shakes beneath my unstable feet,
Stumbling to my knees
I feel the warm water lap, lap lapping over my paws.
Its living creatures scurrying quickly away from my body,
A trail of tears trickles into the water.
I collapse letting it cover me slowly.
Then grasping for breath, I pull myself from the water.

Shiver...

Cold flakes fly, thundering down, dipping trees so
strong
Ground touching turbulence steadied.
Masquerading death meant to be stunning
In the headlights of my car,
Unofficial Finish Line
An Eve
Lady in waiting, Expansive Vagueness
Inconclusive
Bottom Sitter
Covered in white Psychosis.

Screaming Dove

Life is a journey so deeply desired.
It's what we hide from strangers
Who we really are.
Afraid that we will lose what we have discovered,
Look into the screaming dove, the child hidden in the
sand.
Where is she standing?
Sinking, sinking into the dreams of the man at my back
door.
The silence, the weak, the lost, she isn't hopeless, she
doesn't fear
What is taken?
She discovers she yearns for the same, but still wants
more.
The world is lying at her feet. Under the earth she
sleeps, she sleeps.
She doesn't understand, she needs, and needs no
understanding.
Lost under the blue heaven's dew that seeps into her
skin,
She is spinning into the sky losing control of all, of all
misunderstandings.

To un-ravel that the earth is not meant for what people
see. People see.
People see, only what makes them feel safe, they do
not watch they do not look
At what doesn't, please the eye. Pass it by; Pass it by,
look ahead.
Down, down, she is falling,
She is hitting pavement
Headlights in her eyes, tears streaking her face, seeping
into her skin
And
No one looks, no one, looks. The doves scream, the
doves scream.
She is running, running, running, looking back
At the dove
No longer is she crying, she is found, unveiled
Unbroken to the world
She speaks, "You are mine, and we must run."

Once was

Comfort, Warmth, Friendship
Are they here?
I was there, or so I thought I'd been
My tear streaked face, thoughts, possibilities, truth
Slumping downward.
One moment, an action, slight slip up, and you're
alone.
Looking for something lost, shivering, fearful of events
undone.
Searching for an answer
It felt right, you and me.
The time we spent together has always meant
something,
But people like you
Don't hold on to the past for strength, or warmth you
let go,
Like a kite, letting it floats far behind you.
It blurs so that you no longer appreciate what was once
there.
What we had if only for those years,
Moments, seconds, chosen to forget, while I choose to
Remember.

My Angel song

Sing me to sleep
Like a child
Let me weep
Like a girl
Lay my head on your shoulder
Let me curl into you
Help me not to feel blue
Wings of Angels fly,
You've made me
Little thoughts break me
Sitting on the edge again
Simply you hold my hand
All I do is lean into you
Wings of an angel fly
People say goodbye,
Nevertheless, we live a lie.
My eyes want to shut.
Never have I seen this much.
With my head hung down
They say he wore a crown for
Me,
Wings of an Angel fly.
She won't let me die.

I feel myself floating.
I just let it go.
Don't give up now
Yet let it all go.
Wings of an angel fly...
Sit still look at me
You are me,
I am you,
You don't see,
So I let go
Let go...

Falling

The long nights fall like shadows
Covering up my blanketed past,
Hidden in darkness
Quivering from cold
Air blowing through orange sunken leaves
Crunching under feet, warm sunshine
On my face with sweet smells of rain drops
Soon to follow, the fall,
Snowflakes that chill everything, but your heart
Millions of differences, thousands of lies,
Few hopes that are passed among us all
People who live, breathe, die, survive have all known
These thoughts, these feelings
When will it come together, will I, just space out into blackness?
Gloomy days, destructive thoughts,
My tired mind that no longer wants to think,
To move forward, to find something that is fate,
That is reasoned.
Goodness is the light, when you discover it.
I don't know the light.
No one has led me to it.
I know I should long for it, hope for it,
Peace, seclusion cannot be my only amenity let in.
How can I trust again?

Doing it Wrong

It's everything in me
Reasoning, Karma
To fill the void
No where leading me forward
Where I thought I would go
Stupid, stupid mistakes
That eat me alive,
Drowned, partake of me,
Peel me back while you push
Me down
Dreams become repossessed with needs
No longer can we live on ideas.
The realist in me killed my creative desire,
Gorged out my insides,
Replaced
By emotional pain, psychological worries
Spirit, Essence, Lights glow outside this body.
Happiness is in moments, not lasting
Maybe manic, Psycho,
I begin to believe what you think of me,
Analyze what your thoughts conceive of,
Where it places me
Just like everybody else my head screams,

No different than everyone else it seems,
No unique persona, aura,
Intellectual points made slide off my tongue, yet go
silent.
Positioning myself sitting square
I remember you telling me
I sat wrong
Even if it was just a dream
You were telling me I was doing it wrong
I still am.

Deception

Finding Solace
Dreaming in color
Sitting on clouds
Surfacing silence
To gain
Perspective
Away from
Human forms
Regaining solitude
Realizing those I thought were friends,
Feel like foes
Turning to charge
Instead of standing by your side
Telling you
Who you are
Why?
And how?
You need to be alike
And once I thought I was, understood.

Lucidity

What kind of dream are you?
Do you fly?
Do you fall?
Are you above it all?
In the middle, yanked back and forth
Or
Stuck in one place
Glued to one venue
Dumped in a vat of Unforgettable
Void
Do you lose your eyes to get where you go?
Push people in, or shove them out?
Lean, or lean on others?
What do you dream, day after day?
Or
Do they turn away?
After obstacles are placed?
Jump and Jive
Finding balance
Creating dreams from napkins,
Memories re-written
Latter, as we've seen them.

One more Impression

Too much change can burn your inner soul.
No longer recognizable
To those who remember you
Leading to the loss of memories,
History formed to create
Ones that never existed.
Suddenly an enemy,
Frogs dance in your throat as you spin around
Feeling sick to your stomach
At an unbearable angle
You fall gripping
For those thoughts you have left
To keep from floating away
A rainbow in the sky once yours
Disappeared,
That has yet to return,
Illusions made real.
Unexplained miracles, long gone
Friends,
Wishes that never came true,
Waiting at the bottom for the sun to pop up
Warm on my back.
For those to understand what
They never could before
For everything to slip back into place
As a
Balance.

Giving up

Another night of frowning

Crying complaining blaming

Longing to find something outside of this

Of it all

Nothing is ever how I see it

Picture it

Perceive it

Nothing is as I wish

And

Still

I keep wishing

Playing make believe

Dreaming

And

For

What

A disappointing world

In which all is fought

I lay down

To sleep

And wonder when I'll wake.

Part two:

Despair

Nothing Counts

Tonight nothing counts.
My problem is I am mistaken.
Frustrated by this wait dragging on
The more I push it pulls,
Life's obstacles don't stop
After you've hopped, one or two,
I don't care if the fairy tale is over-rated
Or
Unrealistic
It is what all desire.
Even if we say it is not so,
Accepting them with all the pitfalls
Wanting to tear out and edit
Like a good television show.
It's like those nights
Where no matter how comfortable you get
You stay awake.
Life is meant to hurt
That is what so many say.

Outlook

New shoes to walk in
Make me smirk
Not the shoes themselves
Analytically speaking, but a metaphor life change
Hidden
Where has everything presented itself?
Or did I hold back?
The girl in the pretty dress unsure,
Needling idea's till it was stag?
I write
Talk
Re-think
Loading up units inside this person I don't even know
Twitter-patted, frustrated, that I can't go back.
Once I was independent, strong, shocking, ticked off enough to
move,
Now I am just annoyed, sad, depressed at times
Waiting
For someone to illustrate me
Sing with me
Sit with me
Believe in me
Yes, it is all about me
Because it's not.

Questions

Do you want to grin?
Is it hiding inside you?
Like that pout scrawled across your face in crayon.
Doodles etched on sidewalks sick of stalling.
Laugh without pain...
Injury fallen by
A lack of past acknowledgement in a dreamer
Full of distance,
Fed up with her own questions
Practicing Penance in prayer.

Suspended

Snow crunches beneath my feet, steady like things left behind.
Unable to follow the why's, how's, now's and then's
Present time excludes
Lucid
Well structured sound I am not.
Only a boat floating in this water that might tip
Upside down, drowning all hope that fills me,
Livable extended self
Beyond this body
Not knowing any divergence from it.
Never having been detached
Stuck in it
On this earth
Where you can choose to heal, or hurt
Give, or take
Make warmth, or cold
Form ideas's and criticize all.
I sit down on the snow bank, all this pure white, all this nothing
Symbolizing purity like a virgin on her wedding day, or someone
who has never been exposed
Seen as dirty, unclean, immoral.
Tears drip, drop melting the white under my feet. I stand up to
go.
Another day, will soon arise continuing my life.
The tenderness inside me, still in the company of doubt, hate,
Goes on,
One will carry on

Me, moving forward
Until life is gone
I will still weep;
Pain will constantly be with me
Happiness too.
Opposites
That must be, I am.

My chaotic Mind

Why do I run, or even fear?
I should seek you, smile and laugh.
Visions that explode in my mind make me grin.
Seasons changing, time passing, more notches in my belt of life.
Still I run, searching, looking, for more,
Happiness, hope, boundaries, unreachable to my consciousness.
An unseen future
Till death due us part
On earth as it is in Heaven,
I am unconscious of my conscious
Staring at me
Like a wilted flower
Am I dead, or growing?
Have I found, or lost something so deep
To be unconnected
Or
Is the connection still there?
Am I lying too close to the fire?
Afraid that the heat will scorch
My repents
Or that redemption is lost
In my continued state
Of Absolution?

Lost

Not myself,
Rocks of lead fill my body
Weighing me down,
Every sensation, wave, step,
Runs over
Thinking-
Contemplating
Stations of awake, alert
Did I know?
Sealing my eyes shut, stopping to rehearse
Who I was, have been, need to be,
Flying and falling
I can smell, breathe, be clean of what others
Seek judgment upon
Clicking, touching, inventing,
I move on, standing still
All at once stuck in stages
Chilling me
Un-hearing me, diminishing me,
I tell myself it is only what I see
The disbelief is me.

Uncontrollable

No matter, it comes at me.
Like a knife
Without the ice
To dull the pain
I feel it coming,
A two edge sword
Ripping apart
My heart
Tearing at my hope
Shredding my inner peace
All I want is you to take me,
Take this misery
I can't explain
Not of me, or in me, only outside of me
I cannot control.

Rejection

Solace
Useless
Boring
Drowning
Exhausted
Freak
Escaping
Countless
Targets
Irrational
Velocity
Exfoliated.

Observing Me

Lingering isolation,
Purity in strength,
Mixed with hatred, for what I am not.
Little lightening rods,
Bigger demons,
Shut it out.
Me
Un-obscured
Creation met for damnation
Delighting in hours
Not ashamed of my dying flowers.
In the brilliance of it all
Underneath my fall
Everything simple,
Right
I sit here in-between light
While you create my darkness.

Torment

It's tumbling, breaking into clumps
Crashing into my soul, UN-healing my own self.
I've experienced what you have not
Yet forgiven you all.
Still, you say I am going to hell.
You push me down
Weave your web
My mind is pounding so
My heart feels nothing, wish I could cry,
But there is nothing to let go.
Strange feelings I get when life don't seem right.
I move on, act strong, try to hold on, head held high
Always Thrown
Onto the ground, unable to be
What they wanted to see, before them
And
Here I am.
Why?
Now to them what they see is good.
Me, I am still burning, unable to understand.
Why I've forgiven, forgot.
Where am I now?
Who to depend on,
No one.
That's what I've felt. There is no use trying when it all dies.
Wish I could fly when it all dies
Cry: It's what used to show emotion

Words: They use to tell the truth.
Until it all went wrong, never you mind
It may heal in time,
Upon our earth we are given: Hope, Beauty, and treasures
That no one can pry from our fists.

Unforgiving-Forced-Change

Sitting among real people beside me,
Realizing the non-existence pre-texts,
Are more real
Lucid,
Liquid,
Forgiving, then the substance of beings
In existence.
What is imagined grows
More real
Then what is.
Don't try to save me, I already am
Descending inside this me of mine, you want me to pretend
To mold, to bend, to remain condemned?
Little pieces, jag's of shards
Seen
Little pieces pulled apart,
Peace together
Fix my scars
Over with your illusive-ness,
Deep cuts we make,
Emotional, physical, attempting to break
What you want to fix, change
While I close my eyes
To your world
Opening mine
Wishing I could stay.
Outside it's scary

Wanting to flee.
One person sought, one unit
One that doesn't lack,
The Once I was
Slipping under-Not Understood,
My Alice
Lost Wonder
Place your hand on mine
Don't fold!
Lay your cards out to find me
Again "DON'T GO"
Fishtail
Sway,
No outlet it reads,
Undefined
This Alice of mine.

Tainted

I've gone through
Highs
N
Lows
Humming to myself
Pick up, step up
Smile
Focus
Don't lose that Skip
Chin Up.
Let the loss, uneasiness go
Delve into the muck
Let it sink in
Tears flow
I sputter
Surrounded by nothingness.
Gray, blacks, browns, earth smells truth
Hush
Dirt covers us all.

Creating Divergence

I want to rise
Feel better
Discover ways to escape the compromise
Stop the violence surrounding us
End what never should have begun
To get out of these blankets
Holding me down in the comforts of despair
Regain freedom, finding a clique that gets it
Run as if I'm headed in the right direction
Then crash in a park full of natural ecstasy
On the view I'm taking in
To find the change that will lead to
Rebirth
Instead of waking up wondering if
Each step I'm taking matters
But in the end, I'll still wonder
If each moment mattered
And
What did I do to make things better?
For myself or anyone?
I'm still looking for the answer.

Part three:

! Up-Rising!

Public Eyes

You look at me like it isn't real.
It's something I do to pass the time.
The game to move on
Like a goalie
Stopping it, stopping.
I don't halt, I race, sprint, rapidly towards freedom
And you cannot have them, these words of mine.
Imprinted in my depths
United with you, who are tied with me
Every part of you-Is a part of me.
For it is you, who have influenced my world dears.
You who've molded me from our similarity to our
Differences.
We always change
But
We always stay the same.
That is our curse
And
If not yours
It is mine.

! <u>Revolt</u>!

I don't want to hold on anymore, just want to take the fall.
I ain't, No damn Barbie doll. Tired of not being in control, sick of
people saying
Let certain things go,
Not holding on, or trying to change the world is what turns me
upside down,
When you do- it makes me frown. We need the power back in
the people's hands.
Don't you see the corporate control, don't you feel it tightening,
isn't it frightening?
The people you blame are the wrong ones, the things you
pretend not to see;
You say, I am blinded by me.
I am one of the few who see's what others shove away.
I don't want to play, it makes me bawl, you laugh, that's why
I'm feeling jacked,
Like I'll never get the life- I knew back.
Dreaming of who they use to be will never bring them to me.
I cannot find that new click, who really gives a shit.
Where do I go when no place feels like home?
No matter what I do, it leaves me alone.
Don't tell me I can't be bad, or get mad, feel sad.
This is who I am blasting out my views
Punching out fools in my mind
Getting mad that you won't give me the time I need.
It takes so much more now to succeed.
Kicking with the leaves since that way I have no one to please,

Signing those petitions, making decisions about how I'll change the world

You say is fine, I just want to blow out your mind, so far you see

That there is no way you are fooling, or changing me like those I loved.

I saw the change, faith leading them to hate, then preaching peace

Bringing on the heat instead of warmth, fire burns us all.

Tears always fall down my face, but how can they put out your hate that displaces?

Spread your wings butterfly spread your wings bats.

It makes no difference at all, even if you fly you splat!

Never escape, the inability to coexist, you expect us all to do the splits,

Split ourselves into two.

I can't walk in this cold room any more burning, like ice a heat so hot you blaze.

When is it your turn to feel the pain I've suffered, put yourself into my place?

Take my shoes here you go, sit here, do this, do that, eat this not that, worship him not her,

And let me intellectually screw you, mentally deplete you so you'll do your job,

Keep it up so you can pay that cable bill, the only thing to free you still, your mind,

Music has never made me blind; take out your pen start to write again,

Get out that crazy, step up on the bar, the diamond or the pearl, boy or girl,

Trans or bi who gives a -just love me see me -

Fight this system
When they try to push you
Down,
Down
Down...

A heat Wave

All I can say is that I don't comprehend.
Why I cannot be friends
With heat, or the cold,
It's getting old
The fall is never deep enough
Far enough
To climb back up,
Grabbing hold of a wall
Then knocking it down,
Starting again
Building up the fallen
Only to make you trip
Fire Balls,
Burns you up
While trying to lift them
Never good enough to make it
Through the day,
A heat wave
Consistently
Scorching, ongoing, continuing
While I wait for the rain.

~Remembered~

-A Poe-It /Monologue

I am unable to see my footprints in the future. What I have done today may remain past tense, but at times a choice to repeat it due to need. I am human, and to error is my nature. However, in business to error is unacceptable. Power and greed created business.

Bottomless depths, Angles, Turns, Paths, circumferences of my world in mind it is a different Universe. I am a representation of an intelligent being that washed up on a shore where due to a few blurred or damaged cells was deemed unfit for use. Instead of replacing them with new idea's to re-connect the current. It was interrupted with oracles to be used on the lower level of ones imaginations, towards the educational ability of the student, whom moved through the places among pages of words placed on paper to escape harsh realities of individuals who wished to defeat, to take her inner core, crushing all hope, although she lasted longer than they anticipated, morally sound, affectionate, and enthusiastic deeds that should have forced these strengths out of her astral being remained with her. The biggest loss was the assimilation of whom she was onto them. This human girl could not get them to comprehend her soul consisting of a variety of hues.

In fact, I would lye awake for hours daydreaming just to escape the sameness of everyday tasks assigned us. My perceiving was of punishment and entrapment to keep me in my place. When Money=Power, gives privilege, and ensures food, shelter, and security you do what you must, even if it's a camouflaged cage configured by your social leaders. It's why when I close my eyes at night I move, like I moved through papers with words.

When I spoke of where I'd been, the school children of course, it was chaos. The musings of a created reality, our own be sane? It kept me from crashing, going postal-in reality it conformed me. Yet by night I, was free to roam any city, Town Street, with anyone imaginable. Recalling objectives idea's brought forth before I let myself strike concrete chains, still grasping for education that not only would I deny myself, but by allowing fate to take a part unit by unit slowly letting go. Then allowing in what I once pushed out to gain freedom.

I see them, butterfly like I use to songs, friends, like a swirl of rings even with knowledge ensnarement is not always preventable. It devours us encircling our life cycles in wonderment. You think you see signs, a light shining, small embankments, you refuse to believe in the fragments of glass that once cut deep, and the pain is eased; humans forget when it is replaced.

I'd like to think I have not forgotten.

Unsettling

Frustration is beating at my door
Calling
I want to slam it!
I want everything to be released
Push, Run, and Kill.
That's just how it is
An upside down story book,
The piano of my soul
That no longer plays
Striking the keys
Note by note
By
Note.

Sides

I need the willow tree
More than it needs me.
Its leafs cover up-the space, Pace, Place
Leaving me alone.
Materialistic mongers gorge fast
On success, a process of capitalistic seekers.
I hover forsaken
Looking for higher ground
In need of an alignment,
Few contact, seek, linger, edge forward
From this place of betrayal:
Diamonds, Massive homes, thousand dollar dresses,
Desiring escape
Whom on which end?
It trickles down, they say-towards the weak.
We seek vengeance in our voices drowned out by crones
Who hold the people cornered?
Advertisement, Media, Escapism?
Is it really us, whom holds the key, to meet needs?
Are we taken advantage of?
What is your perspective?
Do you fight?
Fall?
Give in?
Weep?
Or do you just continue as they wish you to?
Overrun by what others tell you?

Do you have goals to overcome?
Or have you let them win?
If the meaning isn't having millions, Then...
What it is?
The basis of survival,
Meeting the needs of each person
Without having to give up
Health, safety, and
Stability.
Will you join the parade?
Or wait while nothing changes?

Parts

Pieces...
Balance, weights
Ends
Middles
Extremes
Highs
Lows.
Flowing rivers running rapid,
Seizing up
Stopping
Overflowing
Exploding
Into lights
Nights un-slept
Views unseen
Covered up lies,
That sweats to please,
Ignorance
Darkness meshes with light
No one sees
Instead, they aim
Not to please
Nor do they see
Inside out
The wrapping on the gifts
Illusions
Created to deceive,

Little pieces of me
Scattered about
What you seek out to learn
Now stabs at you gnawing,
Taking pieces of you
Bit by bit, where once hope had constructed it.

Silence in a tired State

Quickly, quietly calm
Without emotion
Dully sitting
Non-repenting
Reflecting extended versions
Of a
Former self
Fluffing, prepping, preparing
Forward drives
In taking
Presence, to be there,
Emoting out what strength
We have left
Blocking momentum of
Undisciplined fools
Lacking an open engagement
Of hope.

No More- Nice Girl

Close them in behind the wall
Make them beg
Make them crawl
No Miss Nice Girl anymore...
You've burned too many of my doors
Trampled on my hope
My life,
Now I'm all alone tonight
The moon shall weep,
I cannot cry,
Lost in the woods
No matter how hard I try
I am unable
Not stable
Emotions stolen by words so sweet,
I cannot deceive
It's incomplete,
So it's time to say
Goodbye...
To look at another sky
So I won't wait for your reply
I won't let you let me die,
Flaming bright my star shall shine
And each glory will be mine.
So I'll leave you behind
Moving forward to find
Each place in which I'll exist,

No, not even a last kiss
For to me,
You don't exist.

Loving Myself

I will follow my heart
Alone.
Hike up stairs
Then slide down them
Stand tall
Shrink fall
Sit, stand, and bend
I will not stop
Nor will I end
Til my last breath
I will take a stand
For who and what
I am.

Meditation

Closing my eyes
Live inside
No one else, watching
Telling lies
Swirling in me
Deeply dug dreaming
Doesn't care what you think
It's all believing
You cannot buy
Digging me
I can drowned in me
If only to be at peace
Creation grown
All my own
Little, small, Medium
Never disappoints.
A ticking clock that never stops,
Stops for no one
My mind stops for no one
If always closed off to be dreaming
This dreaming is me
Keeps me from breaking
Shaking, or taking it out
To a dark place beyond this black
You cannot imagine that
Stillness in the Silence of my own Voice
Voids felt because I have no choice

People never saw abstract
Merely their version of shallow.
I'll always have tomorrow,
Inside myself this truth
Meant for me
Torn apart by social disease
Means
Right
Wrong
Liquid, cream, soft faces
Similes
Warmth, felt for miles
With eyes closed.

You say: "I'm not."

You say that I'm not, I'm not

I've been in places in my head

I haven't been in Bed

You say that I'm not, that I'm not

Each night after my eyes are closed

You are so close, but still they say I'm

Not.

You say its Real life that counts, not these ghosts

Swimming inside me, not the thought

That has grown to guide me.

Little voices in my head

Coincidence they say instead

Two wrongs don't make a right

You can't be mine to miss

cuz, I'm not I'm not.

The Garden I've created

Forbidden fruit

Is nothing but dirt

Sticks and stones won't break my bones cuz I'm not

You say that I'm not I'm not.

Inside my head

I say screw you instead

Inside my head

Always there

Warmth in the light

Guide me tonight

Cuz you're not your not

Anything, but stuck I pray

Cuz you're not who you were yesterday.

My best friend, she is dead, she was not, was not.

An acquaintance instead,

One day it will be

More than this image I see

Are not, was not, is not, will not be

Because everything I know is me.

Out there you are

Sweet star

One to look beyond

To progress,

Then we will not be one less

Instead, we will be

Truth.

They will see, they have no use,

Changing what already is

Instead, it is love they will give

Till then, they'll tell us

We are not,

We are stuck in Salem's Lot.

Unwanted, alone, let us save you

Let us change you.

You say I'm not, I'm not.

I know who I am, I am not listening again

Keeping my truth next to my core

Even in my mind

I will not let your image go.

Take what you can, hold it near

Don't let people take what you hold dear.

Safety that they fear

Let me lay here for years

If inside this head

I am accepted instead

I am, I am, always am

And you love me,

You like me, you need me,

You direct me.

I close my eyes and pray that I'll find you someday.

Contentment

Between awake and asleep
Silent Lucid slumber sleeps
Peaceful,
Restful,
Euphoria,
A Chaotic chance to visit Ghosts.
For them to come in visions
Chasing Dreams
Words of comfort seep from my lips
Dissolving
Artificial flavors
In my own novel
Featuring me
Co-exist in my world.
No exceptions,
Falling down frame by frame
Underneath all the same.
Quit playing all these Tragic, silly, ignorant games
Love is Love
Let them be
What if it was you or me?
Piece by piece I pick me up
Crash
Silently
Sleeping
Mute
Overtaken

In my burrow of bed sheets hidden
Breaking Out
In
Unconsciousness.

Conflicting Views Formatted#
A Poetic Monologue

Praying to make it through more days where stillness doesn't capture me. My moods bite back as I fall into the trap in my head. All around me I see happy people with their beliefs that create ideas of tenderness, strength and union bringing it all together for them. What are you supposed to do? Slowly shoved down your throat, a cold glass of milk straight from the cow's teat told this is who you are to be no questions, told what they know will make you happy as you stand up in defensive anger Not yet having completed the obstacle course put in place, your own device. As if breeding is the only way to take a stance, To be put in place by a man, putting you in a place that everyone else calls freedom, You call torture because he is given the choice; a woman is just expected to bear down, And give children from her womb, love, nurture, peace, All she is while a man can choose. As far as making your sexuality complete mine will never come full circle, if you were to know my needs you would boil over thinking I'd leave your magnificent boy for another warm soft scarlet face warm upon my chest. You don't know the void that fills me, as each one beside me would make it better, two at my side not one, so unacceptable in society. I am alone sitting Indian style in my head where I need to be where I have always needed to be in the shun of it, deep inside my spirit house, tears spilling onto my thighs in the shadowy pale image beside me never to be. My heart says I cannot let you change me, take away me, belittle me, mold me into that, women you still think is a feminist waiting for her call to be impregnated just because she loves a man. Women give, give, and keep on giving while the rest of the world keeps taking from her, all she has given as our mother earth is taken from us by the hand of man, mass consumers, big business, ect. Sucked in like the life that has been sucking women dry for years as we give up our bodies to keep this earth populated by those that keep us down in the corruption of lies. Few lives created into meaning openly pursing light. Me, my view is eccentric, different, side stepped while some view it as an honor I view it as expected. If it were something wanted, not told, then remain the same I would not. My body is my body married or not, my spirit, my spirit, unscathed unchanged without my power to accept, thy change. I swim only in those I wish to swim in with my touch, spirit, and soul, within all of me. You do not choose for me.

Change

The earth tilts, I fall, deepening me
Soothing me
Water trickles over my rocks
Smoothing rough surfaces that once
Made me full of
Greed and vengeance
Now I see it will always be the empty
Space, but I have accepted
What I cannot make mine.
I am me who makes me whole
Only I decide, only I hold,
Only I dream
Only god loves
I may never know of what is open,
Or closed
I may stay in-between uncertain.
It's here inside where they can never reach,
I am soft, I am kind
Only you who, I know not
Who lyes somewhere beneath the world concealed
The path
Help me find it?
I know I must discover who I am.
Be whole before one plus one
Can be, complete
Keep it safe,
Understand do not lose yourself to someone else

Do not fill the black hole to satisfy the passion you crave
You must dig inside deep depths,
Find you
Find you.

Influx of influence

Some voices hold meaning than others put me down.
I grab onto the warmth of little voices thriving with I can,
trying not to give a damn about those that attempt to defile my
plans. The truth inside me does not mimic theirs.
Love and peace, mean equality no matter what you read
or see. Free will has been given open palmed. Hate is not a
tender embrace but a loaded gun held by enforcers backing you
into corners.
Love, I will always see differently.
So go!
Believe as you will but like you I stand firm.
Leave!
Move on to someone else who may be swayed.
The little voice in my head, that's my god.
You have yours now close the door of criticisms.
Let me be.
We're supposed to live in the land of the free..

Part four:

Hope

Faith

In my crazy world, I need time to breathe,
Explore the unexpected
Seek what is beyond me
The things I do not know, hold on tight.
Moving forward I can smile
Brightness surrounds me
I am not alone.
My spirit guide has not left me
Will not stray
I must be doing something right
Every day I pray/Meditate.
Trying to make myself more aware,
Of good things that have been shared,
Amongst: Friends, family, and people I meet.
Wonderment, curiosity will always peek
On mind
Mind it,
It may not always be
Hope will forever be
Inside of
Me.

Thanks

An eager ear to listen
Warm hugs on a gloomy day
Mugs of hot Cocoa
With the tiny little marshmallows
Sadness is pain
You only feel can be taken
By love
Denounced, stripped, from our lives
It follows like a rain cloud.
Good and bad, a balance
A belief
Then calmness
That just stops
Straight lines
Us till it is recycled.

Outside Looking In

Sometimes I slide
I let people see what's inside
My deepest thoughts, fears...
Then I feel the needles poking into my skin.
I'll never win
With words that are spoken.
Then I think of your smile,
It calms me a while
Tears
Trickle down,
I could never frown,
You'll be my mentor
Never leave my side.
Silent, I am lost
The maze twists, then turns
In a world of hate
I don't want to claim
Watching me cry, you turn to me,
Towards me to say:
"You don't have to."

Good night, or Good Morning, whichever you prefer.

Love me
I am falling in love with hope.
Insides bleeding
Sitting next to the stars
That need weeding
Looking for that person, place, or thing.
Damn, has it been that long since I felt like cheering?
Singing, dancing, dreaming?
Watching the sunrise
In secret arms
Uninhibited by ties, or attachments
Anything to feel social
Anything to feel anything at all.
Wanderlust
Twittering on a need to travel
Brainstorming for no reason just thinking
Typing for anyone here willing
Whatever
Chill
Like, oh my gosh!!!
Or
Tears dropping like an emo child
Gothic kid swearing he is, spent of life.
Punk rock fading like a facade
Sneaking peaks seriously
On the music scene
Incredibly unaware of perspective

Searching to complete a sentence
Strings of things
Artistic toys
In pictures
We breed
Gradually tearing down the wall
Of stereotypical social-elites
Similar to
Ground up cow
Trying to force the idea's of peace
On a nation
That creates war
Based on culture
How do we keep them out?
How do we stop the killing?
God is love, yet they kill for him.
My god accepts the unaccepted.
No strings attached father of friendship.
Not isolation
Jailed in a cell
Warm in our beds
At work
Everywhere he is in me
Loving everything I am
We are Rainbows Coexisting
Now it's your turn.

Saturday

In explicit, unconventional, Comfort expandable
What is comfort?
Why do warm arms around us, make us feel like no one can hurt us?
Pursing such escape
To find ourselves in scenarios
With suitcases
Travel light, or winner takes all
Then slide into my sleek sheets
Sporting the pillow
Love commencing thoughts
Hunting for expandable comfort
Effortless
Deep in my sorrow of sinful pleasures
Still pulling it together
In day tearing it apart
Watering down the flowers
Trying to make them spring from
Wilted leaves/petals/fragments
On the way to build up, reconstruct, operate
In full
Searching for that friend, akin to those lost in the past
Said never to find
Found exclusively in youth
Dip, drops, splashes
Dives
Crowds

Here

Just

Once in a life time

God spoke to me,

It wasn't what I wanted to hear

But it is

A little like tripping down a stairwell

Asking for help up

Asking to be held with no strings attached

Begging for a human connection

One of guilt, or not, or just need that fizzles out and pours in

Why is warmth only for lovers? Is kindness not a soft touch?

Or a sly slap on the back,

Witty words, what is it?

Unconditional love is not unconditional

There are always attachments, judgments, expectations,

There is no such thing as things in me.

Hmmmm

Presently, let me slumber, let me chase amenity alone

No mortal will ever relate

I've seen this is how it should be

Maybe, just maybe, one might

Only one

And sometimes

Answers are silent

Immobile

Simple

Startling

Quietly he reads me

His ideas remain buried inside

Unheard
Pushing to bring together both.

More than

Love is more than
Kisses on the beach when you're happy
Its tears when you're sad
Working out late night anger filled frustration
Needs communication
Laughin till it tickles
Talks with tea
Unconditional calm
Celebrating a continuum
Recycled ways to enhance you both
Late night dinners, movies, walks, family ties
Peace by peace the surrender
We've made to each other
Finding ways to keep it tight,
Close, repairing tares like
Tattered robes.

Spirals

LOVE...
TWISTS, TURNS...
CONCEALS...
DELIVERS...
DEGRADES...
DESERVES...
FILLS...
SPILLS...
BUILDS UP...
TEARS DOWN...
IMPASSIONS...
BRINGS HOPE...
FINDS PEACE...
ENDS...
STARTS...
BEGINS...
STATIC...
RECYCLES...
LEADS TO...
HOPE, FAITH,
THAT WILL COME AGAIN,
OR INFINITELY WILL BE
CONTINUOUS...
UNCONDITIONAL BEATS...
TO ONE
PATH
BOUND.

APPRECIATION

The leaves flutter about doing an exotic dance as the wind blows
down my neck.
I admire the autumn display sauntering along the street.
People in cars stare, as if they never had to walk anywhere.
I breathe in deep the coolness of the air, smile, enjoying
sunshine on my face.
Its rays bringing me back to life.
Music, radiates into my headphones out of my disc man.
I take pride in myself strutting down the path holding my head
high.
I let everyone see, right now in the sun I am someone.

Bright side

Hope has never, let me down,
By no means made me, frown
Not at all
Given me lots, and lots of ground
Set me up to be
Everything in me
Little steps, little rocks
Building up these cinder blocks
Built my home
Like a child
Hills I climb
Cracks define me
Water flows through me
Tickle my movements
Nothing is sealed
As forward, goes
Trickles down
Top to bottom
Small sprigs
Blossoms of hope
Yet you mope
I am not up-moved
I am rooted yet flowing
In hope, she sits next to me
Smiles, hugs, a kiss
Acceptance is
Bliss.

Part Five:

Contemplation

Musing

Sometimes we wish to be noticed while others choose to be forgotten. I sit by the old oak, a red book in my hands reading into another world, time passing around me. I stretch out my short legs, small frame, and yawn scanning the landscape, hoping that something will change laughing to myself as if by magic I can will it to happen. Then shake it off to walk down a long road for a cold lemon aid. Air pulls at my hair swirling around my face. I pull it back. I see the store just up a head, small towns are hard to escape, easier to stay, and seek out change in my head rather than facing the fact that I am just too frightened to leave. I walk into the convenience store, dollar in my hand and pick up an 89 cent lemon sugar flavored beverage, pay and stroll out back into the heat of the day. My purse hanging at my side, books in tow. I never go anywhere without them. It's much easier than counting on someone. Then again so is living in my head. Clumsily I open up the bottle taking two large gulps before a breath, analyzing the situation. How did I get here? What happened to all those warm dreams of luxury, pleasant afternoons on the beach, friends surrounding me with kindness, ease, how did I let myself, let them make me happy instead of me, making myself that way? How does one learn to be merry without friends, or rather how to be cheerful with the contacts you have instead of ones, people, whom you wish were your friends? I keep moving this time towards home. I'm sometimes not sure where it is, both places I have lived are quite small, right now this place is smaller. I can run home in less than a half hour. It's a part of my life in which happiness felt like it was "Just around the Corner" like the Shirley Temple Movies singing their way into a content, jolly ending. One of the worst things is not being able to figure out your life, the dots are all there, where is your pencil to connect them? When god gives you a life boat how do you know which one to choose like the right answer to a Jeopardy quiz. Knowing that you have to make some mistakes to discover, develop, divert, continue on...

I grab conviction in what I cannot see, not only in a deity, but in many things, giving rather than receiving in most instances. I receive more from words in books, my lover, family and music, but continue to believe in friends, acquaintances none of us perfect. I finish drinking my sugar; I'm in front of the house. I look at the blue sky, "I wish you were purple." I say opening the screen door to the porch letting it slam behind me.

Angels and Demons

For every act of good, my angels defeat demons,
For every demon defeated one slips
Through the crack, loop hole, fence, agenda,
E.S.P. hanging over my head my, hollow tips.
One false move, trip, side-glance, allowing them in
Without meaning, brings bitterness in sheets
Reminiscent of bubble wrap that you can't see through
Pulling you apart from head to toe,
Right arm to left, like god on the cross
They try to dismantle us, stir us up, make us lose our truth.
So we wonder where God is.
Question our asking of prayers, what we deserve, why so many
people who are evil get away with it.
Why?
This is where I am left, in my pool of pain, where good people
suffer for those of evil intent.
I reach out asking for direction, reflection, understanding, and
forgiveness.
Give me, sanctuary, where I thought none would be found.

Sam

Dear Sam,

The puzzle piece is missing, everything is gone. Did you ever think about the willow trees? Their long leaves flying through the wind? No matter where I've gone the world is all the same. Millions of particles in the air, you could catch a cold. I guess you could die; we'll never get out alive. Are you scared? Me, I am.

The colors of the ocean are the colors of the sand. The book of words that have all the right answers, things that made everything OK, are not among me, only whispers that no longer linger. Things I never knew, I'll never know. Good night, Sam, Good night Puzzle Pieces that never quite fit together. Where are my pieces that fit? Where are they scattered?

Sacred

Is it possible to keep things that are so far from...?
No, it cannot be explained that way
Too obvious
It's more similar to
How do you make things turn out?
Exactly how you want
How do you keep it all from blowing up?
Making it all seem inclusive even if it's not.
To pretend everything is as it should be.
How do you clarify you are special?
Not some messed up maniac
Who doesn't know which way to cross the street?
When it is going straight?
You don't!
You just have to be whatever you are
You have to let society
Worry, not allowing anyone control your action,
But yourself
Don't let them consume your mind.
You must keep it sacred somehow.

Invincible

It's really weird when you want to say something
And
The other person says it first.
In a way it's sort of a relief, everything can be like that.
Trees, Green Grass, Sun Shine, It's been awfully beautiful.
I long, however, for a cold thunder shower, and lightening
I don't suppose it's too much to ask for.
Loads of good things happened today,
Too many, is something waiting to destroy it?
People are like that.
They take what they love and destroy
Without any realization of what they are doing at all.
Some people are extraordinary, and nothing can destroy them.

Frozen Coke

Messages used through our voices travel.
Frozen Coke down my throat
Pieces of cold chunky ice with Carmel flavored syrup
Freezing tenses rising outside in sweetness,
Carbonated
Toxins, in taking pleasure,
Where my unlimited self
Notes
Emotionless
Strings
Attached.

Elusiveness

I don't want to wake up.
My bed is too comfortable.
Dreams are too good.
Reality, is stiff nasty, and meaningless.
As much as you hate it
This truth
It is real
So far those who try to leave reality are considered insane, or
disillusioned.
I suspect we know what is pretend, its meaninglessness.
These fantasies, these imaginings
Eat us alive, if we let them
It kills us-Nagging us to come back.
Considering it is so easy to slide into that place
Where everything is complacent,
A safety net where nothing can harm us,
Silently it does, if we allow it, pulling us away,
Influencing us with the aim reality is not sufficient
Brain washed
Media Frenzies, Feed Illusions of Beautiful people
We are not
On the outside
Deep in my skin
Requests shriek
Tears fall
Laceration is more than a knife making the cut.
It's another Illusion.

I'll never be who I wanted to be; I am just a shadow.

Speculation

What I want isn't something you can hand me.
It's not tangible, only dangling slightly beyond myself.
Past the box that was made to place all of my idea's in
Leaving all the un-redeemed credits that once filled my pages
Incomplete, unassigned, in desposible;
Resembling me
There I once was,
Am not now,
Nor will ever be
Only a soul
Seeking the dream
Inside herself.

Poe-It-Words

Think, Act,
Nothing
Blank
When you have no words
Empty spaces
Remembered actions
Show expressions
Lacking noise
Devoid of voice
In the silence
Sit in the room
Sit inside your world
Sit inside
Blah blah blah
Your lies.

Zone it out-plays it out-breaks!

I hear the beat
A neighbor's music
I zone out trying not to tear at the wall
Drowned it out
Straight talk doesn't work
Never has, when alien boys play the stereo loud
Humbles them - burdening you
Voices speak, you listen, but do not answer
A lot like life, the saying, it is a game and how you play it - is the
answer
Gag me randomly with a spoon, not Spork
A warm blanket is sometimes better than a warm body
My mind is spinning
I am not thinking
In its place, typing current things from my phase
Society can have phases, new beginnings
We can also become deluded by the fibs our mother's taught us,
The media, if we let them run our lives
Bit by bit I blank it out, all of it
Occasionally concealing, it is not there-That their existence is not
the same as mine.
I'm exceptional
Even if I am not understood
My ripples are strong
Someone else will pass them on,
No matter who,
One who has contacted me somehow?

No force is more powerful than the push given by one's self
I kick, scream, run, catching truth continued.

On Repeat

I'm in the gloomy place again, unable to crawl out. One where I want so desperately, what is not mine, as good as a lock on my heart, that no one is allowed to open. Shutting me off from the world I know exists somewhere in space, and time cut off from me leaving me- in despair inside. The only thing I have ever been able to do is pretend, it will all go away. It is not working, it is not erasing thoughts, ideas, and fantasy, things that would take this anguish and replace it with contentment. Words have been my relief, past ability to move forward, adapting to fit, let go, hang out, and go forth, while standing deadlock at the same moment unable. They may hear my needy screams, but not imagine my placement, racing anticipation, emotions, divided into sections unable to be constructed into usable product. Complexity strives to weaken me, solitarily seeing it from views on this hill of mine; peering over a pool of water into my own reflection wondering if you even prevail.

When it gets this way I seek compassion through visions. I want someone to put their arms around me, and make it go away. I am not logical, sinking deeper into my grief, quick sand made by men, politicians; those who think it best to tell you how to live your life. I need to lay my head on your chest while hands, rub my back telling me to Shh and nuzzling as the tears escape my body leaving it yearning for hydration. Myself lying in secrets that make me whole, me expecting someone else to delete torment, guilt, hurt, years of climbing mountains. My face looks at yours, I touch your lips, sigh, stare, you have not turned away, but I still feel lost. I hang my head, defeated. You are not her, and she is not you, as I am not me.

Struggle

Observations, Preferences, Choices, and perception
Never, cloud my mind
I am certain.
It's time that I battle, for the right to gain my worth.
Already I have walked more than miles to reach, destiny
Saw past all the side glances, snide comments,
Remarks that once stung like soap in my eyes
That brought on tears
Breaking me into puzzle pieces,
The devil likes to mix.
Treading water against rapid currents
Praying for peace
Hunting for explanations
Wishing it all would end
Knowing it is his will, not mine
Reminding myself, I am here for a reason.
So complicated, complex, yet perfect
I only yearn for my own.
Small piece of paradise
On earth
Can it be?

An Intervorts prospective

I have always wanted a window seat to sit on looking out into the world to think the most profound thoughts. Depths, deeper than the ocean. That other's would want to look beyond the horizon yearning for more. Instead, I see people resisting, working, giving into the simplicities of living. Nothing wrong with a roof over your head, good food to eat, and bills paid. Still the soul suffers with no passions, desires, art made by the common person for all to share. We glorify the rich. Most proclaiming the rest of us were meant for nothing more. I don't understand the ability to accept it. Marriage, children, family, are supposed to fill these gaps. It doesn't for everyone, some of us want more, fight for it, long for it past what others see. It's not that there is anything wrong with wanting common things, but why shouldn't we move forward, striving for the goals that possess us as we lay our heads down to sleep, our minds race with ideas replaying. That which completes us: Art, words, stories, paintings, dance, and those reaching out to help address social matters usually swept under the rug. I'm tired of the sweeping Maybe we should sweep, the men there holding power kept. Those that pay off the people to contain folks below them not allowing them to rise. When will we resolve things? When will people care? Has feminism been bought, erased, or are we all distracted by the bling? I'm not, and I keep battling with myself not to give up. That someday we will be heard in spite of those who ignore us, denying there is a problem at all.

Part Six:

Acceptance and Renewal

Midnight Express

There is no limit to what we can achieve.
Do such as the dreamers do,
The world is supposed to be open wide to take, do not make
haste.
You the ambition seeker, go-getter, over zealous predominate
girl.
The truth is things don't always go as planned amidst those
curved roads,
Messy family functions, or prickers in the flowers you just didn't
foresee.
The delight spreading fast on your canvas you never knew would
occur.
That smile, it's not for everyone, it's for you.
They don't see how such a silly unwanted pricker of an incident,
One that didn't even make you famous made a difference.
When everyone else is telling you to look elsewhere and
You're wondering why? Where would I go?
This is a home, a dwelling
Known, safe, and providing.

Release

It's a shame, shame, shame, but I'll move on and be good again.
In this deepness that I sink
A query of stony sand
To find my own meaning
Stand again
I don't need the pretenders at my feet
Don't need stress, just release
Let the power go
That has a hold, the one that told me to keep
What could no longer grow.
Don't pressure me anymore.
Don't need the stress, just let it go.
Then I can be whole.
Use to be's, the memories
Left with the change you've sewn
And I accept the separateness,
In which a wall has formed.
I accept it by letting go.
No use in hanging on to something gone.
Let it be, let it be gone.
I don't need pretenders at my feet.
Don't need the pressure.
Let go of the balloon that has already popped.
Broken, separated, changed
Never to be
Filled again.

Peace

The darkness is gone
I can hear the rain
I think, ponder, and create pictures, Memories.
Spoken words
Tell me it's true, I'm seeing
Reality
Not just my daydream, not a world
Of make believe.
Mister Rogers Neighborhood and Saturday morning cartoons
I fall into you.
Close my eyes, relaxing
Unable to comprehend
Everything I have.

Listen

Slap, slap,
Drop, drop
Crash, plunk,
Liquid falls
Gravity pulling it to the roof
As the wind chills me
Trickling down the window pane
Splashing towards the earth it feeds.
Worms squirm to sense the coolness on their bodies.
Deafening sounds Burst,
Animals scurry, flee, shelter on their minds,
Searching for warm hovels to hide in
Stillness.
Slowly birds awaken, as the yellowish warm light rises.
They sing
Chic a de Dee Dee, chic a Dee Dee Dee
Red, yellow, green, blue and a faint hint of purple
Make a stunning background to paradise
Listen, relax, enjoy,
Eden.

Beautiful Fall

Beautiful fall,
Feels like I'm Plummeting
Fragrance of earth and fire
Unite
Blending night chills
An uncommon kindness builds,
First the gathering
Of people
Prayer and hope
Begins the burning,
Offerings of peace,
Approval
Shared
No Shunning or Disowning,
A hold so close
Relaxing,
Non-evasive, nor indigent
Rather serene
Without distress
You are here.

Acceptance

Every Journey takes us.
New idea's fill our heads.
Smiles slowly pane onto lips,
Grace is given.
Time is cherished.
A new beginning,
To stop
Foresee
Unwind
A moment
So we can see the beauty.
Always we must snap back,
To reality
Tic tic tic ticking
Clock keeps spinning
Time's up!
Home
Now facing what was left behind.
Continue
Wrap up
Courage
Never to, run forever.

Realistic Daydreamer

Go ahead and laugh
At the realistic, dreamer,
Have you seen her?
Hair in her eyes,
Everyone else telling lies
Sitting on their thrones,
She is all alone
In her, land of delusions
You find so much confusion.
In it she finds peace
Solution
You make her the victim.
She defines her world.
Comfort conforms her.
While you disown her,
Peace and solution
It brings its own clarification.
Onto her own nation
Not devastation
Others see in her eyes
You just pass it by.
She looks in different windows
And walks through misshaped doors.
She is not keeping score.
Seeking good, in all,
She tries not to let the tower fall.
One you created with all your hate.

In a dream of her own,
She may seek it seems
Little words little thoughts.
Realistic in applause,
Step by step it takes longer.
Turning away the monsters,
Breathing out, breathing in,
Not refusing
Not to begin again
Each and every day
All her own
This soul is her home.

Sunshine

Sensations of being held, with no one near,
Affections glow in anguish,
The middle of sliding,
Into sleep
Slipping slowly
In, soft colors of plenty.
Drifting sweet smells throughout the air.
Little droplets birth random flowers
Springing into my garden
Arranging it all unconsciously
Unpredictable beauty.
We stand, sit, dance and embrace energy.
Composed serene acceptance peaks.
I am a dream
Yours.

ANGEL

Everything
All together
An Angel's essence has:
Great thoughts
High-respect
Shy eyes
Gentle hands
Trust
Lovesick Goosebumps
Picture moons
Many Hugs,
The night would create sun,
And listen eternally.
Realize you're loved.
Seize me!
Care,
I feel stunning.
Soft light
Best friend
Love can't be
Stopped.

Defying the box

Why do we limit ourselves?
We say no, not yes.
Holes in Swiss cheese,
Idea's we never fulfill,
Fear, rejection scrutiny,
Pushing us away from procedures
Leaving it underneath, skin
Crawling along tingling sensations.
We receive what others say, examine, critic and do.
Without reflection,
Choose to question, if only in thought not action.
One life, by way of various choices, leads to numerous
Roads
Devour them all.

It comes back to me

I've tried to be callous when I have been hurt
To not follow my heart
My inner giver
To shy away from forgiveness, I owe myself
Sometimes others
Still, it comes back to me
Like an organ that won't stop playing
The rhythm keeps beating
Forcing me to dance
The tragedies slide by as I sway
Listening to beauty, in the melody
By chance, I meet souls searching
A few stay
Many run
However, I keep playing
Using my chords amongst words
To express
What is inside
Beating my drums
Alone
Along
With
Others
In hope
Always.

Part Seven:

REFLECTIONS

Inner Child
~A MONOLOGUE~

    Sitting in a forest of green all around me among purple hues, I am inching up against a huge tree scanning the horizon, vibrant grass, oaks, pines, and beeches. The lake is before me lap, lap lapping against the shore; listening to the tranquility, as well as intensity, breathing in its spirit I sigh, letting it out again. A squirrel scurries grabbing an acorn, hiding it away for a long winter coming. Smiling, I bring myself upbeat off the ground onto my feet skipping near the lake's edge, pulling up my jeans feeling water beneath my toes. I almost jump back, icy coldness filling my entire body, instantly laughing at myself reminiscing what it was like to be a child, not to hold back, longing for that existence again, playing in the stream as I watch the sun go down envisioning myself back there; I put myself, into an exquisite picture. This is me imagining.

MELISSA JOHN

What can I provide you that you haven't already given me?
Every time I hear "Imagine" by John Lennon,
Your image appears in a pattern of good luck hugs.
You smile for eternity.
No matter where you are now
My junior mint friend
You are forever,
Existing...
Giving me the chance to boycott prom among tubs of ice cream.
Leap in the lake with my cloths on
Or
Trick, or treat one last time.
You gave me sweetness, hope,
An unconditional
Comrade
Always with me.

(This poem was written for a good friend of mine. I will always cherish her, carry her with me. She gave a part of herself to me when she shared her world; the love for the 1960's. She was open, honest, loved all people, and judged not. If we could all be like her, our world would be a better place.)

Images

The words stuck in my mind like velvet crème
Hello, it's like brand new, the world
Velvet crème sky,
Cloudy blue units in pairs,
People in places,
Melancholy faces,
Christmas blahs,
Holiday thrills, chills,
The stepping on ant's that travel up hill.
Resembling little toy soldiers
That were never trained to fight.
It doesn't last right?
Walking through thoughts, endless thoughts
Never brought to life
Hmm ha ha little toy trinkets
It seems when we were children
All had such dreams,
Visions, we gave up on
And
Stepped on like glue sticking to our shoes,
Defeated
We listened to them too
Allow them to suck us right in.
Pray
Trust that someday maybe
Little toy soldiers will battle
And grown ups will keep on dreaming.

Dreaming, dreaming, falling, fallen, deeper
Into, all dreams shared long ago,
Accept it
Permit it to settle within your core.
More profound than everything
Rapidly commit to memory
Childhoods past.

A gift to remember

I remember when my brother and I were snug in our beds,
Tales of the world were read.
The Secret Garden, with cranky old Collin
Are you afraid of the dark? I was at the start.
My, *The cat in the hat,* mother didn't like that.
In Green *eggs and ham,* I was Sam I am.
I remember when the library wasn't my friend
And the summer reading program
Mother enrolled me in
But I don't recall the books I read.
I do remember a tall, medium sized, curly black haired woman,
A teacher who helped me learn to love to read
The babysitters club, Ribsy, Sweet Valley twins,
And whatever else I could uncover
I remember how I felt I might fly
With *Harriet the spy* among her colorful notebooks:
Green, red, purple, blue and black.
I respect the gift that was given,
And
The books I have to read,
I will open.

The Perfect People

The perfect people scare me.
Make me feel alone.
I've betrayed the perfect people,
Standing on my own.
Everything seems blurry, a mass of silver gray.
I wish I could escape here, to find my perfect day.
But everyone is laughing,
Pushing, pulling hard,
And I am feeling empty.
Full of loneliness and scars,
You are here beside me.
I don't want to lose.
The perfect people frighten me.
Everything goes dark.
Which way do I move?
Which way do I choose?
Beside the perfect people?
Or
Beside you?
And when the blackness fills me everything is gone.
An when the cards are turning,
I am running fast.
I will escape this planet.
I will leave at last,
But only when I'm ready.
When everything is fine.
Right now I am not prepared; I can't escape my mind,

The perfect people gone (NO!)
The perfect people live.
And everyone is dancing, everyone is hid.
Hide me perfect people, hide me in your sight.
I've given up my dreams; I've given up my rights,
But first I wish to say.
I said I wish to say!
That the perfect people, are not perfect on any sort of day!

Childhood

Hello side walk
That I've tread upon.
I've drawn several pictures
On your slate.
Sometimes you bring back memories
Of a content small child
Drawing on your face.
You never complain about the weather,
Or even the slightest change
Going on around you,
You are just cold, wet, cement
That somehow
Once brought me happiness.

For my Grandfather

Attempting to recollect moments that flew
Sharing days by means of a motorcycle ride,
I can see clearly, a picture in my mind
Accordion playing polka,
The old 8 track player living in the living room, and an organ,
As kids we played Frisbee tag,
You were providing a safe haven.
Always cookies/snacks
At the end of the day
Chats amongst grownups.
We grew older.
Riding in a parade with
You
In the Javelin:
Waving, grinning, proud
Like I am to have been loved by you.
Supportive of my decisions
Understanding obstacles I faced
You too were proud of who I became
Both of us persistent in life to meet our goals.
You graduating from high school to turn out to be a tool and dye
maker,
Me with college, graduation, full time employment, and poetry,
Poetry I am sorry I never shared.
Intertwining our lives
We learn from each other,
Give and take

Giving back, what you gave us.

Enchantment

Love is insightful, whispers change
Crawling up walls
Discovering new dimensions
Emotional beauty, drawn on paper.
Resembling rose petals,
Feeding on memories like drugs
Past all the
Chaos
Tripping on hope
Completely
Smiling beside the man, exhaling despair
Breaking free
To be open, uninhibited
By pain
Solitary
Seeing more
Mirrors face forward
Light on dark
Sparking my imagination
Setting down a novel
Tears split splat,
Then I curl up in my pillow.
Atop a heap of laundry
To sleep on my illusions created by inspirations.

The Purple Dragon players

I was a drama kid
With a big sweet smile.
I was a star for a little while,
Yes, I was,
The world, it sang to me.
All my aspirations,
They set me free.
That was then my drama queen,
That was long ago.
Where am I my drama queen? I wish I could know.
I lost her around the curves and bends along the road.
I found something that took its place,
Something I couldn't let go.
I miss the days of life
When I was someone else at night,
Stage lights in my face.
If even I wasn't the center,
Lie down, relax a bit
It's not everything
Remember, it's not,
You are
Everything
The drama queen could not be.
You are still
Free.

Going home

The entirety of this room of mine has been taken out as if it is
devoid of me. I could have never existed here, lived, breathed,
hoped, fantasized, or made memoirs so full of bold perspectives
that they missed. Home is no longer a connection, or
attachment,
Reminiscences
Are
Stepping back is impossible
Whilst none of you is left
Similar to the people, who've gone on,
On the way to do better things
While I still hear the girls on the sidewalks
Screaming at fireworks, racing, grinning, in love with the
Idea
Of what's next
Before time and change
S
E
P
E
R
A
T
E
S
Us all
Me still holding vivid
Images inside
Others push away

An inquisitive writer
If all I can type from is experience
Passions, ETC
What good am I?
This emotion of rain fall
Except nothing follows
Wanting to re-connect
A social circle
Once engulfed me
In college, high school, no longer seems possible.
Tight knit binding buddies so deeply felt gone
Changed
Depleted
Rarely staying intact
Like the warmth that home
Once brought you.

Touched

Souls meet without contact
Lonely to be in your embrace.
The veins, my heart that pumps blood
Through my body means nothing,
Impossible
Without the body, there is no heat,
Wishing two souls as light could meet,
The heart is not love
It doesn't feel love
It is only an instrument
Only the spirit feels love
Our lives slowly die each day
Hold me?
Make it cease
Only leading back, back, back
To birth from death.

Individuality

Must I ask questions everyone asks?
Am I weird since I color?
My freakish hair covers my eyes.
I spit watermelon seeds on the ground,
Admire the sun, moon, and stars
Staring at things from odd angles.
Should my view be narrow?
Choosing only to drive down the straightest highway?
What's wrong with roads that veer off, or obstacles?
That make it, all what it is
Emotions that either build us up
Or destroy us
It's not really what your parents have made you,
But the way you choose to mold yourself.
Often something that really makes you change,
May be something you feared yourself.

Forgiveness

Forgiveness means you are, the bigger person.
It doesn't always mean they will forgive you.
It's letting go of the past.
Opening up doors to your future,
It's a release not to carry it in your heart any longer.
A dead weight you lug,
Given to God to handle,
Forgiveness is something you do for you.
Not the other person.
Not all people can forgive
I am learning.

Leap of Faith

My life is a leap of faith.
It's all based on timing,
Not on our success or trying.
Right hemisphere, wrong hour,
Misplaced goals, and disconnected power
Felt during movement, turning slowly
To complete an unseen
Declining dream,
That never seems to come
We continue
Slow progressive acts
Falling down
Stumble
Get up
And struggle
For what?
A LEAP OF FAITH
Taken, in ourselves
Challenges, worth risking, sacrificing time
No easy way to finish the task
Trick, not looking back
Concentrate, focus
Grasp it in your hands'
Like it lives!
And
Jump!

Epilogue

Be kind, gracious, loving,
Inspire
Motivate
Gain wisdom
Coexist with each other
Put his, or her shoes on
March into another realm of existing
Seek out similarities within
Look beyond
Difference
Embrace them,
Hope, you have it in yourself
Accept the unaccepted
Accept yourself.

Author's note

This is my social suicide,
My pride,
What I am within,
A chance to open, unlocked doors
To reveal me to you,
Those who have no clue.
Will you still fancy me?
Will you tell me to bugger off?
As the English say
I suppose a few will ask me to stay.
Poetic puzzle pieces firmly in my grasp
Thrown out for your enjoyment, your judgment of each moment
Suspended in time
For all to see
This is every part of me.

Please check out my blog for more poetry at:
www.controversialrebelwritersheart.wordpress.com

25094611R00085

Made in the USA
Columbia, SC
02 September 2018